Providence, Rhode Island

New England

New England

By ROBERT WENKAM

RAND MCNALLY & COMPANY
Chicago · New York · San Francisco

Other Books by Robert Wenkam

How to Photograph Hawaii
Text and photography by Robert Wenkam

Micronesia: Island Wilderness
Photographs by Robert Wenkam, text by Ken Brower

Hawaii
Text and photography by Robert Wenkam

Micronesia: The Breadfruit Revolution
Photographs by Robert Wenkam, text by Byron Baker

Maui: The Last Hawaiian Place
Text and photography by Robert Wenkam

Kauai and the Park Country of Hawaii
Text and photography by Robert Wenkam

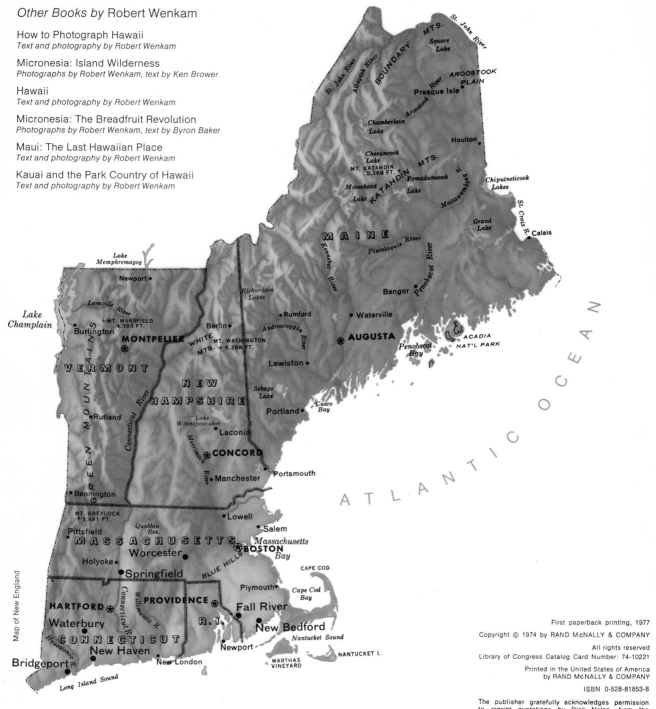

Map of New England

Book design by
MARIO PAGLIAI

◀ Springfield, Vermont

First paperback printing, 1977

Copyright © 1974 by RAND McNALLY & COMPANY

All rights reserved
Library of Congress Catalog Card Number: 74-10221

Printed in the United States of America
by RAND McNALLY & COMPANY

ISBN 0-528-81853-8

The publisher gratefully acknowledges permission to reprint quotations by Dick Nolan, from the *San Francisco Examiner;* transcript of Will and Ada Urie's interview, courtesy of Vermont Historical Society. Material from *What the Old-Timer Said* by Allen R. Foley, by permission of the Stephen Greene Press, copyright 1971 by Allen R. Foley.

Contents

New England Is My Adventure   6

WHERE IT ALL BEGAN   7

The Yankee Merchant   23

REVOLUTIONARY COUNTRY   25

NUTMEG COUNTRY   39

The Connecticut River Valley   43

THE BERKSHIRE HILLS   49

The Way It Was Is Best   55

THE GREEN MOUNTAINS   59

A New England Kitchen   67

THE WHITE MOUNTAINS   79

*"It's Workin' and That's
the Main Thing to My Mind"*   85

LAND OF THE POINTED FIRS   91

A Sampler of New England Life   99

THE ATLANTIC SHORE   107

Land of Two Worlds   111

New England Is My Adventure

I'D LIKE TO ACKNOWLEDGE the thrill of discovering New England—the land where American independence was born—and the excitement of meeting the past in close proximity to the present. Where 100 years ago is merely yesterday. Where the bridge at Concord town still smells of burnt powder, and I once thought I saw Paul Revere's horse tethered to a split-rail fence on the Lexington Post Road. Where tiny village homes cluster around white steeples like friendly groups of country folk crowding a church bazaar.

I've found it most exciting to be in New England. To contemplate my impressions of a landscape and a people, trying to pull together kaleidoscopic images—old and new—received through the window of my Mustang as I rolled along the turnpikes and side roads of the six states—Maine, New Hampshire, Vermont, Massachusetts, Connecticut, Rhode Island—that make up New England.

And while on this journey, I inadvertently discovered something about my own heritage. My name is spelled wrong—Wenkam should be Wenham. The Wenham Historical Society kindly transcribed several old letters in their files and revealed a fascinating genealogy to me.

Baron de Wenham had arrived on the south coast of England to fight with William the Conqueror at the Battle of Hastings in 1066. The Baron founded a town, south of Ipswich, and Wenhams still live there. Wenham, Massachusetts, twenty miles north of Boston on the way to Gloucester, is named after the town in England.

When I learned that pioneers left Wenham and Hamilton towns for the Northwest Territory in 1787—founding Marietta, Ohio, on the way—I was even further intrigued because I know Wenkams, or Wenhams, who live in Ohio and Indiana. Investigating further with the zeal of a detective, I uncovered the original of my great-great-grandfather's birth certificate. On it his mother is identified as Mary Gage, a native of Montreal—the hometown of Maria Theresa Gage, daughter of British General Thomas Gage of Revolutionary War fame. By any measure New England is where coincidence and history come to life.

I only found one unfriendly native—a strange creature who forced his way ahead of my car in a gas-station line in Montpelier, Vermont. The friendly natives, found in every state, are too numerous to be listed, but I would like to name a few who were especially helpful.

Elizabeth and William Ballard of Norwich, Vermont, fed me the best food I ate anywhere in New England. It was easy to understand why Mrs. Ballard's baking sold out first at church bazaars. Bill's library was very valuable for browsing and researching.

Two friends from Greenwich, Connecticut—Robert Wallace, *Time-Life* book author, and Sam Pryor, retired vice-president of Pan American—shared bed and bread and much information. Pryor has a superb antique doll collection, and I enjoyed Wallace's marvelous stamp collection.

Close to Boston live Franklin and Emily Goldblatt Patterson, who put me up for the night in their remodeled Cambridge cottage. Emily personally showed me the traditional sights on Beacon Hill.

And far up north in Phillips, Maine, Laura and George Appell talked about Maine and Borneo over lunch.

Overnight visits at Anita and Gary Soucie's Norfolk, Connecticut, residence were always an education in New England conservation. He authors widely published articles on environmental issues, and she writes children's books.

I must also give credit to the various New England newspapers that accurately report the news and what's behind it. Some of these are the *Boston Globe*, the *Rutland Daily Herald*, the *Maine Times*, the *Vineyard Gazette*, and the *New England Sierran*. I enjoyed the well-edited *Yankee* and *Vermont Life* magazines.

A photographer is somewhat like a sculptor who chisels away what doesn't matter, leaving behind what does. I approached my New England book assignment in much the same spirit—to discover the essence of this historical land and then photograph it.

First I purchased a small collection of books on New England, but as I began reading and driving around the six states, I found many contradictions between what I read and what I saw and so I stopped reading and decided to discover what New England was all about with my own eyes. I think it worked out better. I was less influenced by what other authors and photographers thought important. I could take pictures of what I liked best, not just repeat what had been done over and over again or what somebody else thought was the traditional thing to do. As I looked at some famous lighthouses, for example, I recognized photos that were in a dozen books and fully expected to see three tripod holes where previous photographers had already taken their pictures. I was pleased I could do it my way.

Most of the contradictions I sensed while driving from Vermont to New Hampshire to Maine and southward could be explained by a disparity between the romantic view of New England voiced by summer residents and foggy travel writers and the starker reality of the day-to-day life of a people who work for a living at the factory, on the farm, or in a small leaky boat pulling up lobster traps. To me an old rusty hayrack was not picturesque—it signified poverty and failure. An abandoned farm was sad, and I didn't want to photograph unhappiness.

I've photographed what I like and enjoy—what I think is great and wonderful about New England. But even then it is only a sample. There are not sufficient pages to reproduce all that is worthy, all that is beautiful and worth remembering. I only hope that what I have shown here will add one more voice to those who are trying to preserve the beauty and heritage of New England—for this is the only New England we have. I like it.

Cape Cod shoreline

Where It All Began

In a remarkable restatement of the Pilgrims' first years in the new world, costumed local people reenact the year 1627 at Plimoth Plantation, an imaginary reconstruction inside a wood fortress originally designed to protect the pioneers from hostile Indians, but today equally effective in excluding contemporary urban America. It is a long step backwards into history 350 years ago, after the Pilgrims had survived their terrible first winter with the help of friendly Indians. The Mayflower II *(a replica built in England in 1957)* rests at anchor off the summer resort of Plymouth, where Plymouth Rock marks the traditional landing place of our forefathers.

Plimoth Plantation, Plymouth, Massachusetts

Plimoth Plantation, Plymouth, Massachusetts

Replica of the *Mayflower*

Mystic Seaport, Connecticut

11

Tillinghast Pond, West Greenwich Center, Rhode Island

Cordgrass

Watch Hill, Rhode Island

Watch Hill, Rhode Island

Old Sturbridge Village may be the largest antique collection anywhere. That is the way it started, when two local brothers, Albert and Cheney Wells, realized the extensive collection of artifacts deserved more than a glass case in a conventional museum. They began collecting old buildings to exhibit their treasures of another era, and it soon became apparent that reconstruction of an entire village would best display the heritage of the first fifty years of the Republic. Old Sturbridge Village became the re-creation of an imaginary representative New England community dating from 1790 to 1840. The visitor who remains from dawn until dusk experiences a working day of 150 years ago in a living tableau of American history.

Old Sturbridge Village, Massachusetts

Old Sturbridge Village, Massachusetts

Walden Pond, near Concord, Massachusetts

"Then to my morning work. First I take an axe and pail and go in search of water, if that be not a dream. After a cold and snowy night it needed a divining-rod to find it. Every winter the liquid and trembling surface of the pond, which was so sensitive to every breath, and reflected every light and shadow, becomes solid to the depth of a foot or a foot and a half, so that it will support the heaviest teams, and perchance the snow covers it to an equal depth, and it is not to be distinguished from any level field. Like the marmots in the surrounding hills, it closes its eyelids and becomes dormant for three months or more. Standing on the snow-covered plain, as if in a pasture amid the hills, I cut my way first through a foot of snow, and then a foot of ice, and open a window under my feet, where, kneeling to drink, I look down into the quiet parlor of the fishes, pervaded by a softened light as through a window of ground glass, with its bright sanded floor the same as in summer; there a perennial waveless serenity reigns as in the amber twilight sky, corresponding to the cool and even temperament of the inhabitants. Heaven is under our feet as well as over our heads." —Henry David Thoreau, Walden

20

Statue of Roger Conant in Salem

House of Seven Gables, Salem, Massachusetts

The Yankee Merchant

NEW ENGLAND is where American independence was born. Where Sam Adams presided over the meeting that led to the first violent display of civil disobedience when patriots disguised as Indians dumped British tea into Boston Harbor. The colonists in the South devised early political ideologies for our embryonic democracy, but it was the ingenious Yankees of New England who shaped the nation into the industrial-political complex we know today.

Through mechanization and the application of innovative technology, the rugged New Englander changed his cottage-handicraft economy into an industrial machine that determined the future growth of the young nation to a far greater extent than rambunctious political ideas. The invention of mass-production techniques revolutionized manufacturing and provided impetus for developing a laissez-faire economic system and unrestricted exploitation of manpower and natural resources. In a way it was the New Englanders' interpretation of the biblical exhortation to "multiply and subdue the earth."

By royal edict New England colonists were not allowed to migrate westward and open up new lands. They stayed where they were, forced by rugged terrain and long harsh winters to live close together in compact villages and continue their association with the sea as a source of livelihood. The necessity of utilizing all of the limited natural resources gave the people, in the course of several generations, an expertise in environmental adaptivity that provided unique opportunities which they quickly seized. Their severe environment molded political philosophies that were later crystallized in the U.S. Constitution and at the same time created a merchant establishment and an expanding economy that guaranteed the success of independent government. Colonists benefited from the luck of an early start in discovering trade opportunities for manufactured goods, developing methods of selling the products, and building fast ships to transport them across the oceans. Soon New England manufacturers were trading in a wide range of salable products, from cookie cutters to shoes, and profiting handsomely on every transaction.

The farmer who made a few extra door latches during the long winter often sold them cheaply to a roving peddler who in turn sold them in villages farther down the valley. Sometimes the handyman with a talent for hammering metal or fabricating small hand tools would pack the brass and tin goods on his own back and travel long distances to sell his wares in isolated communities. He later became well known as the "Yankee Pedlar," and his visits satisfied the need for such common necessities as cowbells, platters, hinges, spoons, knives, locks, and round metal balls to put on the ends of sharp ox horns.

The peddler who was far from home with no reputation to uphold sometimes indulged in what became known as a "damn Yankee trick" and sold basswood hams, white-oak cheeses, and wood nutmegs. Despite the fact that nutmegs only grow in the tropics, Connecticut is still called the Nutmeg State—a probable tribute to the shrewdness of early Yankee traveling salesmen who by creating a market helped establish the basis for manufacturing in New England.

Sometimes enterprises started manufacturing with very meager resources. At Southbridge, Massachusetts, William Beecher built a small mill near a stream and with four hired helpers ground lenses for eyeglasses and simple telescopes. When the small stream dried up during summer droughts, he used a horse for power. On one occasion he paid the strongest man in town ten cents an hour to take the horse's place and generate all the power necessary to operate the mill. Today on the same site, now extending for half a mile along a branch of the Quinebaug River, is the flourishing manufacturing plant of the American Optical Company, employing 10,000 local residents.

For more than 100 years, New England geography nurtured the growth of commercial and industrial activities. The numerous streams of southern New Hampshire, Massachusetts, and Maine draining into the tidal estuaries of Rhode Island and Connecticut provided not only year-round waterpower but also easy access to the ocean transportation that brought raw materials ranging from cotton to whale oil from distant shores.

New England inventors provided technological leadership, and their inventions whetted the consumers' appetite for material comforts. The political establishment, organized into town halls and commonwealth general courts, eventually became the public machinery utilized to license expansion of profitable business and to provide democratic forums to regulate their excesses.

Salesmanship and product promotion were not neglected by New England manufacturers. Advertising acquired its unique American flavor when Boston merchants used the embryonic press to quickly sell the varied products imported from marketplaces around the world. While honest value for the dollar and "money-back guarantees" were good ol' Yankee traditions, many a new farmer in the Far West was still occasionally stuck with questionable merchandise by a shrewd "Yankee Pedlar" who had just left town.

In Lynn, Massachusetts, a young female entrepreneur bottled her home-brewed medicinal compound for women suffering from "Female Complaints or Disorders." She called the much-sought-after medication "Lydia E. Pinkham's Vegetable Compound." For almost 100 years her popular beverage was sanctioned by influential women's groups until the Federal Pure Food and Drug Act of 1906 required that contents be identified on the label. It was only then that the Anti-Saloon Leaguers and Woman's Christian Temperance Union activists learned their favorite remedy contained a good percentage of alcohol by volume.

Easy sources of waterpower shaped the landscape of New England as investors searched inland for waterfalls and streams to harness. Small mill towns sprang up wherever sufficient current was available to operate a waterwheel. On every river and stream draining the 180 lakes within twenty-five miles of Boston, hundreds of small businessmen erected factories to manufacture a thousand different products. Some factories became giant enterprises that still prosper today on the same site. Others, like the extensive Amoskeag textile mills in Manchester, New Hampshire, vanished in the depression years after decades of profitable operation.

Of great interest to the fledgling manufacturers in New England was the exciting news that machinery for spinning and weaving cotton had been invented in England. Export of this machinery and even engineering drawings of it was prohibited, but Samuel Slater, an Englishman, went to work in the new textile mills, studied their operations, memorized machinery details, and then sailed for the United States with his head full of everything needed to start textile mills spinning. In 1790 financial backers advanced Slater the money to construct his first mill, located in Pawtucket, Rhode Island, and powered by the Blackstone River. Within twelve years, twenty-nine other mills were started by traders using Slater designs and financed with money from whaling, rum, and slavery.

Francis Cabot Lowell investigated millsites on the Merrimack River in northern Massachusetts, where he planned installation of power looms on a large scale. In 1822 a group of Bostonians invested in his proposal, and Lowell—the town he had picked before his death as the location for his mill—became a company town that housed and fed its employees and even buried them in company-owned plots.

Farther north the scramble for millsites with river-power potential converted the rural New Hampshire communities of Nashua and Manchester into booming mill towns. The swiftly flowing Merrimack River was walled in behind narrow red-brick mill buildings—some a quarter mile long—backed by rows of drab worker tenements.

Europe watched in amazement as the small New England towns rapidly grew into great industrial centers, astounding economists and overseas commentators. Irish, Polish, and Greek immigrants joined with French Canadians to fill thousands of jobs offered in the mills, changing forever the makeup of traditional New England from dominantly Puritan Yankees to a new ethnic mix of Europeans speaking a half-dozen languages and importing as many different native cultures. French, Polish, and Greek newspapers appeared. The Greeks dominated such a large section of Lowell that the city came to be called a modern American Athens.

Yankee capitalism proved to be as efficient in exploiting women and children as it was in inventing the machines for its employees to operate and the time clocks for them to punch. Most employees worked over eighty hours in a six-day week for $5 or less. Women were paid half the weekly wage to work the same schedule. In the 1850s when single male Lowell power-loom operators earned an average of $1.75 a week plus meals, a family of five required about $10.37 a week for the barest necessities. Even then wages were generally paid in company scrip honored only in company stores, which charged exorbitant prices. Entire families were forced to work merely to stay alive. Young children, deprived of any schooling beyond elementary grades, worked long hours at demanding tasks and were paid even less than their parents.

Mill owners enjoyed increasing prosperity while employee working conditions deteriorated and the disparity between wages and living costs widened. Inflated currency following the 1849 California gold strike and steadily increasing prices for food and clothing took their toll of foreign immigrants who received little assistance from local authorities in their quest for improved working conditions and civil rights. Annually more than 3,000 Massachusetts laborers were imprisoned for debt.

When 800 mill girls in Lowell struck for higher wages, public support dwindled because of their "blatant feminism." By 1911 when a Massachusetts labor law did reduce weekly working hours for women to fifty-four hours a week, the industry retaliated by cutting wages. Within three days most of the workers in Lawrence, Massachusetts, were out on strike.

Twelve militia companies—later augmented by infantry and cavalry—were called to duty in Lawrence. The picket line swelled to 20,000 workers, and violence was directed against the strikers. Children were dragged to jail with their parents. But this violent confrontation between strikers and company management eventually resulted in the first victory for mill labor, who won wage increases, time-and-a-quarter for overtime, and an end to the discrimination against union members.

Many years earlier, in 1699, Edward Ward had described New Englanders for the future historian: "The Inhabitants seem very Religious, showing many outward and visible signs of an inward and Spiritual Grace; But tho' they wear in their Faces the Innocence of Doves, you will find them in their Dealings as Subtile as Serpents. Interest is their Faith, Money their God, and Large Possessions the only Heaven they covet." Edward Ward had adequately assessed the spirit of management in New England—as well as the rest of the industrial United States—that was especially evident in the late nineteenth and early twentieth centuries and led to labor strikes throughout the country.

The ingenuity of New England craftsmen directly influenced the nation's growth far beyond the Green Mountains of Vermont. The famous Wells Fargo stagecoaches were designed and constructed in Concord, Massachusetts. The first covered wagons carrying families to settle the Northwest Territory departed from towns that were part of the original Salem Plantation. These pioneers founded Marietta, Ohio, en route, defending themselves against Indians with the Sharps rifle, invented in Windsor, Vermont. This deadly weapon was later responsible for wiping out the buffalo, source of food and hides for the Plains Indians; it also enabled the settlers to invade Indian lands with impunity. It was the Henry repeating rifle that helped Union troops overwhelm Confederate positions in the closing days of the Civil War. Shocked Confederate soldiers spoke in alarm of the rapid-firing rifle as "that damned Yankee rifle that you load on Sunday and shoot all week." Also of New England origin were the Colt revolver and the Winchester rifle. Eli Whitney of Massachusetts produced interchangeable gun parts using assembly-line methods he devised, thus becoming the father of mass production.

The inventors of New England comprise a fascinating ledger of ingenuity and inspiration. Their names read like a "who's who" of American industry. A New England sampler of inventors would have to include Samuel Hopkins (pearl-ash manufacturing process), Joshua Stoddard (horse-drawn hay rake and steam calliope), John Deere (Moline steel plow), Gustave Franklin Swift (refrigerator car), Thaddeus Fairbanks (platform scales), Isaac Babbitt (Babbitt metal), Elias Howe (sewing machine), Samuel F. B. Morse (telegraph), Robert H. Goddard (liquid-fuel rocket), Charles Goodyear (vulcanization of rubber), the Stanley twins (Stanley Steamer), the Duryea brothers (the first American gasoline motorcar), William Stanley (transformer), and the Rogers brothers (silverplating).

To New Englanders goes credit for such useful items as square-bottom paper bags (Luther Crowell), detachable collars (Ebenezer Brown), standardized clothes patterns (Ebenezer Butterick), wallets (Dana Buxton), creases in men's pants (John Simmons), and men's garters (F. Barton Brown).

The challenge of the sea was always a ready lure for courageous New Englanders. Whaling fleets out of Nantucket Island and New Bedford fished oceans from Antarctica to the polar seas and ranged across the Pacific Ocean on three-year voyages for valuable sperm oil and whale bone for ladies' corset stays. In 1768 tiny Nantucket Island boasted 125 whaling ships and exported whale oil to England.

The New Englanders who stayed home found their challenge in conquering the problems of an increasingly complex society by inventing new techniques and machinery that helped bring the United States into the industrial age.

Wayside Inn, South Sudbury, Massachusetts

Revolutionary Country

Dogwood

Boston Public Garden

Tremont Street, Boston

Minuteman statue, Lexington, Massachusetts

Concord Bridge, Massachusetts

Newburyport, Massachusetts

Longfellow House, Cambridge, Massachusetts

Paul Revere House, Boston

Old North Church, Boston

Harvard University, Cambridge, Massachusetts

View of Back Bay, Boston

Pryor House, Greenwich, Connecticut

Nutmeg Country

Congregational Church, Norfolk, Connecticut

Greenfield Hill Cemetery, bordering the crest of a long ridge rising from Long Island Sound, may have been used as an Indian burial ground long before the first white settlers arrived. It is said the Indians gave early settlers permission to use the cemetery only if new graves were dug no more than four feet deep to avoid disturbing the remains of the Indians buried earlier at deeper levels. Town records identify three soldiers buried here as having fought in the French and Indian War, and local people claim more Revolutionary War soldiers are buried on Greenfield Hill than anywhere else in Connecticut. The oldest gravestone is dated 1737.

Greenfield Hill, Connecticut

Tiffany Farm, North Lyme, Connecticut

The Connecticut River Valley

THE FOURTH CONNECTICUT LAKE is the first lake. Perched on a steeply sloping hillside near the Canadian border, the Fourth Connecticut Lake, 2,600 feet above sea level, is the source of the largest river in New England—the Connecticut River. The river runs from its source in a southerly direction forming the boundary between New Hampshire and Vermont and continues through Massachusetts and Connecticut to Long Island Sound—some 400 miles—and has a drainage basin 280 miles long.

White-tailed deer, black bear, elk, moose, and caribou roamed the Connecticut River valley, and each spring the river shimmered with the Atlantic salmon, American shad, and striped bass on their annual spawning runs. The caribou and elk are now gone, eliminated by some 300 years of land clearing for agricultural development and industrialization. Some moose may still be found in the wild northern sections of Vermont and New Hampshire where their habitat has been least disturbed, but Atlantic salmon were eliminated long ago by dam construction on the Connecticut River and steadily increasing pollution along the river's entire length. Only shad still make an abbreviated run upstream, entering the river's mouth at Old Saybrook on the Connecticut shore.

Algonquian Indians called the long river, tidal for a considerable distance inland, Quinatucquet, and it is this name that evolved into Connectecutte and then Connecticut. The Dutch explorer Adriaen Block rediscovered the river in 1614 and built a trading post on the site of present-day Hartford, Connecticut, thus claiming a broad territory for his native country. English settlements followed in the 1630s, and finally after a brief conflict in 1650 between the Dutch and the English, Dutch traders were forced to abandon their claims to the river and the valley.

Connecticut colonists manifested their spirit of independence at an early date by obtaining a colonial charter that allowed them considerably more freedom and independent action than most of the other American colonies. When it appeared to the king of England that the long-neglected colony was going too far in its pursuit of liberty, the king's agent—Sir Edmund Andros, governor of New England—moved to revoke the charter and called on colonial officials to surrender the document. As the meeting began, windows of the town hall were suddenly flung open, and a gust of wind blew out all the candles in the room. In the ensuing confusion, the charter was spirited away and hidden in a large oak tree nearby. "Charter Oak," as it was called, became a symbol of freedom and independence for the Connecticut Yankee.

Meanwhile, problems were developing between French settlers in Canada and the English colonists. The Connecticut River served as a useful waterway for the French and their Indian allies to raid isolated villages and settlements established by English colonists.

Probably the most famous and successful raid ever mounted by the French and Indians against these farming settlements occurred on the northern Massachusetts frontier. Over 300 French and Indians, commanded by Major Hertel de Rouville, pounced without warning upon Deerfield during an extremely cold winter in 1704. They burned most of the town, killed forty-nine residents, including two children of the Reverend John Williams, one of New England's leading Congregationalist clergymen, and took more than 100 prisoners.

For almost four weeks the captives trudged northward through deep snow to Montreal. Many did not make it. The wife of Reverend Williams was tomahawked when she could not keep up, and when their few-week-old baby proved too difficult to care for, an Indian bashed the child's head against a tree. But Reverend Williams and his seven-year-old daughter Eunice survived. Two years later Williams was allowed to return to Massachusetts. Eunice, however, having converted to Catholicism, remained behind and married an Indian.

The raids were partially avenged in 1759, when Robert Rogers, leader of the famed Rogers' Rangers, sacked a village of the marauding St. Francis Indians and fled from his enraged pursuers down the upper Connecticut River to a fort near present-day Charlestown, New Hampshire. The capture of Quebec by English forces and the signing of the Treaty of Paris did much to bring peace to the upper valley, yet small groups of Indians still remained resentful of the white takeover of their lands. After the Revolutionary War 300 Indians joined an English lieutenant to terrorize Royalton, Vermont, in a wild spree of plundering and burning isolated homes and farms, slaughtering cattle, and taking white prisoners.

English colonists were schooled in self-reliance by many teachers, including the Indians and the rugged environment they chose to settle. As fishermen they fought probably the worst storms generated along the shores of any ocean. As farmers they fought natural forces to clear a small piece of earth on which to make a living. As interlopers they fought to wrest a continent from the native inhabitants. The English Crown arbitrarily gave the settlers the legal right to settle on the Indians' land, and they drew up their own laws to guarantee their property rights.

Geographer Russell Smith characterized this conquest "as a shameful story. I should hate to defend the white man's end of it before the Creator of Mankind."

Three of the valley states—Connecticut, Massachusetts, and New Hampshire—were among the thirteen original colonies that created the United States in 1776. Vermont held out as an independent republic, not joining the fold until 1791 when it became the 14th state in the Union.

In the far upper valley a small group of settlers held out still longer. Three adventurers from New Hampshire acquired a large tract of land from the Indians and carved out their own country. In 1832, when New Hampshire officials tried to bring this territory within the state's jurisdiction, the residents formed the Indian Stream Republic and appealed to Washington for recognition. Washington bluntly informed the upstarts that since they were within the territorial limits of both the United States and the state of New Hampshire, they should stop this foolishness. But they continued in the characteristically stubborn manner of New Englanders, however, and did not abandon the attempt to establish an independent nation until 1836. Even so, it was perhaps the smallest and shortest-lived nation ever known in the Western Hemisphere.

Commercial interest in the Connecticut River valley began with the Dutch, who had early founded a substantial Indian trade dealing in furs and other goods. English settlers from Plimoth Colony were attracted by the rich soil and temperate climate inland from the Atlantic shore and were the first in the valley to build permanent villages and to raise livestock and farm produce. As the population grew, shipbuilding, fishing, and lumbering became increasingly important, and soon tanneries and small local mills thrived by processing leather, grain, lumber, and paper.

With the development of mechanical equipment in the early 19th century and the widespread application of ingenious Yankee inventions and manufacturing techniques—including interchangeable parts, which led to assembly-line production—New England's machine-tool industry mushroomed. Factories making a wide range of articles from guns to pumps to sewing machines used the river both as a source of power and as an economical way to transport raw materials and finished products.

In 1785 the first bridge spanned the river between Walpole, New Hampshire, and Bellows Falls, Vermont. The 365-foot-long bridge was built as a business venture by Colonel Enoch Hale, who collected tolls based upon the number of horses pulling passenger or freight wagons. Residents of the upper valley, who sought ways of traveling downstream around the falls, prompted construction at Bellows Falls in 1792 of the first canal begun in the United States. A series of nine locks carried barges, rafts, and small steamers around the falls. The nation's second and third canals were also constructed along the Connecticut River, farther south at Turners Falls and South Hadley, both in Massachusetts. The river, while originally navigable for its entire length from Long Island Sound almost to the Canadian border, is interrupted today by a series of sixteen hydroelectric dams, commencing at Holyoke, Massachusetts. Only the locks at Windsor Locks, Connecticut, are still open to small vessels.

Residents along the Connecticut River have always assumed their river to be the birthplace of modern shipping since John Fitch, the inventor in 1787 of the first American steam-propelled vessel, was born in Windsor, Connecticut. In 1793, fourteen years before Robert Fulton's steamboat, an improved version of Fitch's boat, with a steam-turned paddle wheel, was launched by Samuel Morey at Orford, New Hampshire.

The Bellows Falls canal inspired plans for steamer service the entire length of the Connecticut River, and in the early 1830s a passenger and freight packet especially built for the new service sailed up the Connecticut River to Bellows Falls, arriving to the accompaniment of town whistles and considerable enthusiasm by local residents. The ship was anchored downstream for the night while the great event was celebrated. In the morning thousands watched while the captain carefully guided his gaily flagged ship slowly into the first lock, only to belatedly discover that the side-wheeler *William Hall* was too wide for the locks. The trip was never repeated, and after 1840 the railroads had eliminated all commercial river traffic.

Over fifty colleges and preparatory schools have been founded in the Connecticut River valley. Many of these—Dartmouth in New Hampshire; the University of Massachusetts, Smith, Amherst, Mt. Holyoke in Massachusetts; and Trinity and

Wesleyan in Connecticut—have gained international renown.

Dartmouth College has its origins in a religious seminary founded in Lebanon, Connecticut, by Reverend Eleazar Wheelock. The purpose of the school was "saving the souls of savages." Reverend Wheelock noted at the time that the Indians were rapidly being run off their lands and that "the work must be done at once if any Indians are to survive to be saved." His idea was to remove the Indian male from the "irregularities and laxities" to which the pupil was exposed living at his tribal home and to surround him with the influences of the Puritan home and church. Wheelock also boarded Indian girls so his students could return home with a spouse properly schooled in cooking, sewing, and a fear of God.

But Reverend Wheelock wanted to expand, and when one of his students went to England and succeeded in raising a considerable endowment for the Indian charity school, Wheelock decided to relocate in Hanover, New Hampshire. The new school's charter, granted in 1769 by King George III of England, established a college "for the education & instruction of Youth of the Indian Tribes in this Land in reading, writing & all parts of Learning which shall appear necessary and expedient for civilizing and christianizing Children of Pagans as well as in all liberal Arts and Sciences; and also of English Youth and any others."

But it soon became apparent that the Indians did not want "christianizing," and Dartmouth, although never becoming famous for educating Indians, did become one of the finest educational institutions in the United States.

Mear Farm, Greenwich, Connecticut

State Capitol, Hartford, Connecticut

Yale University, New Haven, Connecticut

Housatonic River, Connecticut

Thames River, Groton, Connecticut

Williamstown, Massachusetts

The Berkshire Hills

Pond near Norfolk, Connecticut

Congregational Church, Litchfield, Connecticut

Whately, Massachusetts

Garlo House, Westhampton, Massachusetts

The Way It Was Is Best

HEN THOMAS J. MESKILL, governor of Connecticut, announced he had ordered a major revision of controversial plans for modernizing the four-lane Merritt Parkway into a high-speed expressway with eight lanes, he was acting in the best tradition of a long list of New England leaders who at one time or another have tried to stop destructive progress that has scarred much of the countryside and leveled many of the historic sites and buildings.

"I took a look at the plans in horror and sent them back to the showers," said the governor. "They would have changed the basic nature of the parkway, and I can't allow that. The Merritt Parkway is one of the country's most beautiful, and we want to keep it that way. The people concerned about this project were right, and the designers were wrong."

President of Save the Merritt Committee, a Fairfield County stockbroker said of the governor's decision, "I'm delighted and overwhelmed. This is what our group has been fighting for six months, and it proves you don't have to have court suits and demonstrations to make this system work."

The citizens' group had just won another supporter in its fight with the promoters of economic growth at the expense of cultural values and community integrity. The highway-department plans to widen Merritt and to construct a major interchange for the new U.S. Route 7 at Norwalk are literally paving the way for a projected super expressway slicing upward through some of the most beautiful and historic landscape in New England—across western Connecticut and Massachusetts and up the entire length of Vermont to Canada.

A worse desecration of New England scenery and farmlands could hardly be imagined. This jigsaw conspiracy by three state-highway departments to put together a new north-south freeway without arousing the ire of local citizens is testimony to the "highwaymen's" capacity to thwart public will. It is symbolic of the politicians' instinctive drive to expend federal tax monies regardless of whether the projects they recommend are needed or not.

It was necessary to obtain two court injunctions to halt construction on Route 7 in Connecticut and Vermont because highway officials failed to file adequate environmental-impact statements as required by law. It is obvious to many residents that the new highway will dominate patterns of land use and population growth in the rural landscape it penetrates, covering the farmland with second homes and undesirable strip development.

"Improving" U.S. Route 44, which traverses the state from east to west and connects with Route 7, would tear a corridor through the small community of Norfolk in northwestern Connecticut. The proposed route, designed to make it "unnecessary for heavily loaded trucks to pass through the center of town," will ruin homes and carve up some of the most beautiful scenery in this part of the state.

Norfolk residents who object to this unnecessary damage to their community are countered by the highway department with a threat to widen the existing highway through town, a plan that would pave the town Green and bulldoze away the giant elms in the central park. It is argued that the new highway alignment will encourage "economic development." This issue has divided Norfolk residents many times during the town's futile attempts, over the years, to industrialize. Today Norfolk

is a quiet residential community of gracious homes, summer music festivals, and one small factory assembling fluorescent starters. It's the kind of place New England is all about.

It's not that Norfolk didn't try to be like the industrial town of Manchester. In 1760 the town fathers could boast of four sawmills, a gristmill, a blacksmith shop, and a tannery. Ten years later two iron forges were in operation. During the Revolutionary War an ambitious scheme—that ultimately failed—involved several busy Norfolk ironworks in the production of one-foot-long bar-iron links used in a giant chain barrier stretching across the Hudson to prevent British ships from sailing upriver.

Abundant year-round waterpower at Norfolk continued to attract various entrepreneurs, and increasing demands for manufactured products ushered in a short-lived industrial era. Numerous factories, erected along Blackberry River and Hall Meadow Brook, produced hoes for southern cotton plantations, axes, shears, furniture, scythes, pistols, and wagon axles as well as silk hosiery and cotton shirts, pants, and dresses.

The Civil War brought prosperity to Norfolk, but with the postwar development of steam engines, the old waterpowered plants closed down one by one, and Norfolk gradually resumed the slower-paced life of a primarily agricultural community. But farming never was too successful in Norfolk, with its poor soil and profusion of stones and rocks in the fields. One early visitor remarked on seeing Norfolk for the first time, "I never was out of sight of land before."

The railroad builders came to Norfolk in 1864 with plans for constructing the Connecticut Western Railroad, an east-west railroad to connect Hartford with points west via Norfolk. They touted the railroad as "the only thing that would prevent its [Norfolk's] becoming practically an abandoned town." Later to be given the prestigious name Philadelphia, Reading and New England Railroad to boost stock sales, the promoters promised to build a railroad station in the center of town to help overcome opposition. Their plans called for construction of tracks across the town Green via a cut 100 feet wide and over 20 feet deep. The route stirred up considerable controversy among Norfolk residents.

Most townspeople wanted the railroad on any terms, because of the new factories that would surely follow. Few of the opposition spoke up until Reverend Joseph Eldridge, described in contemporary newspapers as a man who had "won the love, admiration and respect of his people by the beauty of his life and character and sterling intellectual ability," expressed his concern. The railroad cut would have crossed the town Green directly in front of his church, forcing the removal of many fine elm trees, the Civil War soldiers' monument, and the center of Reverend Eldridge's vegetable garden.

The minister was joined by an influential merchant, Robbins Battell; but most others, even those with misgivings over losing the town Green, remained quiet, feeling they would lose the railroad if they opposed the route. Without Reverend Eldridge's strongly expressed opposition and leadership, it is doubtful if the town Green would exist today.

Reverend Eldridge fought against the proposed railroad route on the grounds that it was unnecessary and would wantonly ruin a beautiful park that had "always been dear to every true-born Norfolkite. In opposing this lay-out across the Green," he argued, "I am not prompted by any desire to carry a point simply for the sake of carrying it. I deeply regret the necessity of opposing the views of so many of my fellow citizens, with all of whom I have the most friendly relations. I do it because in my judgement, I am required to, in order to promote their real and permanent interests." He sounded like a leader of the New England Highway Coalition opposing Route 7. "The railroad across the Green would cost the company somewhat less," continued Reverend Eldridge, "and being nearer straight, would as a piece of engineering be more perfect. We can have a good practicable railroad around the Green . . . but it will cost the railroad more. They proposed to take the route across the public Green without paying anybody anything for the right of way."

Reverend Eldridge spoke often, opposing the use of public parklands for economic purposes and defending the right of "this poor little town" to preserve itself. He apologized in eloquent pleas from the pulpit, saying, ". . . I must trouble you with a few remarks on the value that many of us attach to the Green, and the injury that must accrue to the town if it is defaced by a railroad track . . . running through it from end to end amid clouds of smoke and dust, many times a day. This public Green is an heirloom and inheritance. It was laid out by our fathers, and they planted these grand old elms. It is central to this town . . . it is a pleasant gathering place where the people assemble to worship God. . . . It is a safe pleasant playground in one part; in the rest, shade and tranquility. . . . The most enlightened people in the towns around would regard the sacrifice of our Green as an act of barbarism. The work of destruction once done is done forever."

Following numerous hearings and public recriminations between railroad promoters and Reverend Eldridge, the town Green was saved. Engineers reluctantly sharpened the curve entering Norfolk and bypassed the Green on a slightly longer route after appointed railroad commissioners in three separate meetings denied the railroad's request to take the proposed shortcut across the Green. The commissioners related as a last point in the stormy arguments that they objected to "establishing a precedent for running a railroad line through any public park." Norfolk had their railroad and their park.

In press accounts at the time, there is nothing to indicate that Reverend Eldridge was publicly thanked or even noticed at the celebration held on the town Green when the first train arrived in town. The businessman incorporator of the railroad received a gold watch with the following engraving: "Presented to E. T. Butler, Esq., by the citizens of Norfolk in recognition of his services in the originating and completion of the Connecticut Western Railroad."

The first train arrived at the tiny Norfolk station in 1871 to pick up and discharge passengers and load aboard Norfolk's unusual pineapple cheese, so called because of its pineapple shape. At this time the cheese was the town's chief export. The few remaining sawmills kept busy making cheese boxes. The promised industrial boom never did arrive, but the adverse factors that had hampered the industrial and agricultural development of Norfolk ever since its founding—the rocky hills and deep forests—became valuable assets in the eyes of new visitors who arrived from New York and other metropolises on frequent railroad excursions.

By 1900 Norfolk had become an important summer resort. Farmhouses solicited "summer visitors," and Norfolk's hotel catered to increasing numbers of guests escaping New York's summer humidity. Residents from other parts of Connecticut discovered Norfolk's pleasant surroundings. Mark Twain came up from Hartford for two summers, riding the train that was supposed to bring industry.

Wealthy people began to see Norfolk as the perfect site for summer homes. The railroad spotted private railway cars on special sidings while their rich occupants scouted for old homes and farms to purchase. It was the wealthy summer people who built the school and library, and one wealthy Norfolk resident established the Yale Summer School of Music and Art on the grounds of an old family estate. These affluent summer residents substantially changed Norfolk community life into the mix of cultures and relaxed living found there today. The house servants and gardeners they brought to Norfolk for the summer stayed on, and their descendants remained in town all year.

Soon the working middle class also came to Norfolk and remained there year-round to enjoy the benefits of country living. Before the development of the automobile, it had been difficult for young men to both live and work in Norfolk because there were few jobs available in the town. But the increasing use of the automobile as the everyday mode of transportation made it easy for young men to commute to jobs in other towns. They worked in Winsted, Torrington, Hartford, and Waterbury; some even went as far away as New Haven.

And so Norfolk people forgot about industry and decided pleasant living was indeed an asset—an asset they could best develop by keeping Norfolk just the way it was. The railroad ran its last train through town fifty-five years after its first run. Ten years later, in the middle thirties, a New York scrap dealer pulled out the tracks and shipped the scrap iron overseas. The beautiful town Green is still there. Norfolk had spent almost 200 years failing in everything but being itself.

Tobacco drying, Connecticut River valley

Tobacco, Connecticut River valley

Montgomery, Vermont

The Green Mountains

Northern Vermont dairy farm

60

Moss Glen Falls, near Granville, Vermont

North Hartland, Vermont

63

South Royalton, Vermont

Post Mills pond, Vermont

A New England Kitchen

ASILY SEEN across Barretts Field from the center of Norwich, Vermont, the residence of William Ballard nestles against a hillside where Meadowbrook Road forks just beyond the new bridge. Historians place its construction at the time of the Revolutionary War, when great hand-hewn timbers supporting a high-pitched roof and eighteen-inch-wide floor planks were common building materials in the remote upper Connecticut River valley.

The Ballard house was surely one of the better farmhouses of the day. But like many other old homes, it suffered indignities over the years—particularly during its decade as the Happy Hill Tavern, a sort of country tearoom and occasional inn. It was rapidly deteriorating when Elizabeth and Bill Ballard called the owner on a winter day in 1939 and asked the price. They moved in, sleeping on the floor downstairs while they restored the interior.

The kitchen is the gathering place of the Ballard home. Bill removed the awkward porch added in 1925 and opened up the original kitchen fireplace on the north side of the central brick chimney. This fireplace, covered over since 1850, is nine feet in width and almost high enough to walk into, with built-in oven complete with all the hooks and cranes that the isolated farmer's wife needed for cooking. Where the old butt'ry (side pantry) had projected from a north wall, the Ballards added a kitchen more suited to contemporary housekeeping, with a new pump over the well and a wood-burning range ordered from the Sears Roebuck catalog. In 1940 Elizabeth's mother sent them an English Aga coal-burning range for Christmas, and it is this stove that today dominates the room and most of the activity in the Ballard kitchen.

A dozen ornamental plants—among them patience, begonia, African violets, oxalis, amaryllis, geranium, potted rosemary, a bunch of tarragon, and sprigs of Italian parsley filling a blue glass pitcher as well as some stragglers Bill rescued from a swamp—crowd the sill of the window overlooking the meadow. Potted ivy has been trained up each side of the window and meets overhead, softening the window frame so that there seems to be little difference between inside and outside.

Mrs. Ballard has the ability to produce superb dishes from the most ordinary of foods. She can't remember when she evolved her homemade bread recipe. Her bread is considerably heavier than the chemically laden supermarket variety, yet she uses fewer ingredients. I watched her make it.

MRS. BALLARD'S WHITE BREAD

46 ounces milk	2 tablespoons salt
2 tablespoons chicken fat	¼ ounce package dry yeast
4 pounds flour	

Warm milk and chicken fat together until fat is liquid. Mrs. Ballard always keeps a supply of chicken fat left over from Grange chicken suppers on hand and says, "Nothing else measures up to it—except perhaps duck or goose fat. You must add the fat in small slivers so it melts before the milk is too hot. If too hot, the yeast is killed." Yeast should be "blood warm," she explains, "the same temperature as newly milked milk." It doesn't matter whether the flour is bleached or unbleached, and Mrs. Ballard adds more salt than usual and omits sugar—"to bring out the wheaty flavor."

Pour melted fat and milk into the bread mixer and add the salt and yeast. Stir and wait three minutes before blending in the flour with a long-handled spoon. If using an old-fashioned model bread-mixer pail, "take fifty turns." Otherwise stir until smooth and let rise for three hours. Then twist another fifty turns or knead by hand the equivalent and let rise until doubled in bulk. Divide into three loaves and place in greased pans. Cover with towel and let rise above top of pans or "when it bumps the towel." Bake at 350 degrees until nice and brown. Immediately upon removing from oven, brush melted butter over crust and set aside to cool.

When cooking in a coal or wood stove, the temperature in the oven can decrease during the required baking time, which may also vary. Thus to produce an even crust, it is necessary to move the bread pans around to favor the hot part of the oven.

Mrs. Ballard tells of the country housewife who asked her husband to watch the bread while she stepped next door to the neighbors, "telling him to put the front pan in the back after the back became brown and take them both out when they were done." When she returned in a couple of hours, she found the bread burned to a crisp. Talking to her neighbor about it later, she complained, "It's terrible what these men do. After all, all he had to do was set and remember."

The skills practiced in Mrs. Ballard's kitchen may really be what is called "New England cooking," for the individual artistry involved in blending salted and smoked meats and vegetables grown on remote subsistence farms into three daily banquets for a hungry family surely must have taxed the inventiveness of even the most inspired cook. By sheer necessity the New England cook of yesterday was more creative than her ancestors in England, France, Germany, or Italy.

The New England settlers were not prepared for the wilderness in which they found themselves. In this new land they discovered foods that were strange to them—tart cranberries from the cape bogs, syrup from maple trees, and pumpkins, blueberries, beans, corn, wild turkey, deer, and clams. The Indians were a big help to these early settlers, teaching them such useful things as how to fish for the abundant cod and how to plant corn. They showed the newcomers how to prepare certain foods; for example, how to combine corn and beans to make a dish called succotash.

Using what this new land made available to them, the housewives in the New World became adept at creating recipes that were an ingenious combination of the old and the new, thus developing the American style of inventive cooking.

The New Englanders put together beans, salt pork, and molasses imported from the West Indies and called the concoction Boston baked beans. They took the bread the Indians had taught them to make out of corn and rye meal and added molasses to create a marvelous brown bread to serve with the beans. Apples were made into dumplings, sauces, and pies. Native beach plums, huckleberries, blueberries, blackberries, raspberries, gooseberries, and currants were blended into jellies and used in making muffins and puddings. Stewed cranberries were served with turkey. Strawberries were spooned onto shortcake and topped with whipped cream.

The pioneer housewives brought variety to basic menus by using pickles, jellies, and chutney. Aromatic roots were added early to simple farm dishes by cooks constantly searching for ways to enhance routine meals. Sassafras was a common substitute for nutmeg before clipper ships bringing spices direct from the East Indies made pepper, sage, mace, paprika, and cloves as common on pantry shelves as homegrown parsley, chives, and thyme.

From the efforts of these settlers have come foods that are recognized as being typical of this region. Some of these dishes—like the traditional corned beef hash and New England boiled dinner—have become northeastern institutions. But to most people, New England means oyster stew, the clambake, and clam chowder.

Many Rhode Island and Connecticut housewives still insist upon tomatoes in clam chowder while the rest of New England scorns the idea. A Maine politician is reported to have said that the use of tomatoes undermines "our most hallowed traditions" and suggested that cooks adding tomato be forced to "dig a barrel of clams at high tide" in repentance.

NEW ENGLAND CLAM CHOWDER

1 quart shucked clams	⅛ teaspoon pepper
¼ pound chopped salt pork	2½ cups boiling water
1 large finely sliced onion	4 cups scalded milk
4 cups diced potatoes	4 tablespoons butter
½ teaspoon salt	

Clean and split the head of each clam so that it is open flat. Remove grit and black cap, using 1 cup cold water. Separate the soft part from the firm part, saving a cupful of the softest parts, and chop finely the hard body portions. Cut pork into small pieces and render until crisp, adding onion. Fry five minutes and strain into stewpan. Parboil potatoes five minutes in enough boiling water to cover. Then drain and cover bottom of pot with potatoes. Add chopped clams, salt, pepper. Dredge generously with flour before placing another layer of potatoes, spices, and flour. Pour in 2½ cups boiling water. Cook everything for ten minutes; then add milk, soft parts of clams, and butter. Boil ten more minutes, watching for any scum to form. If it does, skim it off immediately. Add butter and push stewpan to back of stove for about an hour for the chowder to "ripen."

Should you desire Rhode Island clam chowder, you may add 1 cup stewed and strained tomatoes at your own risk, but Rhode Islanders are better known for their ritual clambakes, an integral part of summer days on the Narragansett shore. Indians first showed the settlers how to do it.

The first requirement of a New England clambake is many extremely hot rocks. Prepare a fireplace by alternating logs with rocks the size of a man's head until there are about five layers, depending on how many hundred people are eating. The fireplace should cover about six by five feet. It will take about two hours to burn down. Along the New England shore from Maine to Connecticut, heaps of empty clamshells identify places where Indian tribes gathered for clambakes, but nowhere is there any evidence of the correct ratio of rocks to guests. Indians originated the shellfish feasts, and while later residents elaborated on the ingredients, the essential idea remains unchanged—cooking clams, fish, corn, potatoes, and lobsters over the clam and seaweed steam generated in a hot-rock oven.

The hot rocks are separated from the ashes with potato forks and pushed into a square. Rockweed, a common local seaweed, is quickly spread over them and covered with a wire mesh. In rapid succession clams are layered atop the mesh, followed by another layer of rockweed, then potatoes still in their skins, onions, fish in cloth bags, small sausages, corn on the cob, and whole lobsters. A heavy, wet canvas is secured over the steaming pile, and after an hour or so the rockweed and clam steam permeates everything with a mouth-watering odor. First course after lifting the canvas is always clams, accompanied by a cup of melted butter and a mug of beer. A knife and fork are never used.

Life on the frontier of New England, where just staying alive was a routine achievement, inspired a great variety of stimulating and fortifying beverages ranging from basic apple cider to exotic combinations of local ingredients. When sailing vessels began trading with the West Indies, merchants imported molasses to convert into rum. Evaporating maple syrup and distilling rum became flourishing enterprises and an important part of the social and economic life of New England. Distillation of rum became a major industry, and rum was exported in large quantities to Africa in exchange for slaves who were transported to the West Indies and later to the southern states. Large quantities of rum were also imported, but the rapid development of this import business did not diminish the New Englanders' special enjoyment of their home-brewed liquor, which still retained quite a considerable reputation of its own. When important friends dropped by or an extra vote or two was needed, the prized jug was brought out of its storage place in a secluded part of the cellar.

One local concoction was called metheglin, a variety of mead originally made in Wales. Depending on how much is needed, to each gallon of water stir in 3½ pounds honey and boil forty-five minutes. Put a handful of bruised walnut leaves, about two ounces to the gallon, into a wood keg and pour in the boiling-hot mixture of honey and water. Let stand overnight before taking out the leaves. Add a piece of toast on which a cake of yeast is spread and let stand for three days. Close bunghole of the keg with a sandbag and let the liquor stand undisturbed for three months before drawing it off into bottles or jugs and corking. Ordinarily metheglin is made in late July, so it's ready to drink during political campaigning.

Some of these country liquors were quite potent. An old story told of a New Hampshire farmer who was carrying a jug of applejack along the railroad tracks and was caught in the middle of a trestle with trains approaching from both directions. Frightened, he dropped the jug—which was full—and it exploded, blowing up the bridge, wrecking both trains, and killing all the fish in the river for several miles in each direction. Survivors could find only the stomach and gullet of the farmer. Those organs, because of an almost continuous diet of applejack, were so heavily lined with copper that when they were sent to the mint, they realized $14.30 in pennies.

When repentance seemed due, the pious housewife might look upon the Bible as a cookbook, just as sometimes the cookbook is one's Bible. From the village church bazaar comes this old recipe inspired by biblical knowledge.

VERMONT SCRIPTURE CAKE

Judges 5:25 (1 cup)	Genesis 24:20 (1 cup)
Jeremiah 6:20 (2 cups)	Isaiah 10:14 (6)
I Kings 4:22 (3½ cups)	Leviticus 2:13 (a pinch)
I Samuel 30:12 (2 cups)	Exodus 16:31 (1 tablespoon)
I Samuel 30:12 (2 cups)	I Kings 10:2 (to taste)
Genesis 43:11 (1 cup)	

Combine in order of the biblical references and follow Solomon's advice for making good boys (Proverbs 23:14): "Thou shalt beat him with the rod, and shalt deliver his soul from hell." Mrs. Ballard says, "A good cook will know what the temperature of the oven should be."

Farmland near Springfield, Vermont

Church flea market, Brandon, Vermont

Farmland near Vershire, Vermont

Rock of Ages Quarry, near Barre, Vermont

Lake Dunmore, Vermont

Lake Dunmore, Vermont

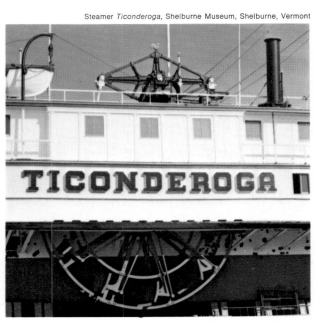

Steamer *Ticonderoga*, Shelburne Museum, Shelburne, Vermont

Sugar maples

Farm near Lyme, New Hampshire

Second Connecticut Lake, New Hampshire

The White Mountains

Dartmouth College, Hanover, New Hampshire

Mount Chocorua, New Hampshire

"It's Workin' and That's the Main Thing to My Mind"

ABOUT TWENTY-FIVE MILES south of the Canadian border on the gentle rolling hills beyond Glover, Vermont, is the small farm belonging to Will and Ada Urie. They were both born within a few miles of their home. The Uries represent a New England life-style—with its traditions of hard work and rugged individualism and its link with the past—that is rapidly disappearing. It is a good feeling to share Will and Ada's thoughts.

The following interview was taped in 1973 by Wally Hubbard for the Vermont Historical Society in Montpelier:

"Where were you born, Mr. Urie?"

About three miles over here on the Beech Hill. You been up over Mr. Williams who owns the place there. The barn's gone down now, but he's a summer resident and he has the farm now. And wife's always lived in Glover over here in the center of town. And so that's as far as we've ever been.

"Do you feel part of Craftsbury or Glover?"

Oh, Glover, yeah. We do all our business this way. We're the last one that goes to church in Craftsbury from this way, then it divides and they go to the Glover church from here down. But we've always went to church at East Craftsbury. So we stuck to it here. It seems to be the farming was our only hope. And it's eleven years since we retired halfway. Come from the other farm out here and we brought six cows with us so's not to be homesick, but it's worked out. They can support us. We have thirty acres of land here. We have an egg route and we sugar and wife cooks for the campers and we can exist right on this thirty acres of land without touching our social security then. And I think . . . ain't nothin' ailin' the farmin', if you can do that, is the way I feel about it, it's workin' all right.

"What was a small six-cow farm like when you were a young man? Was it any different from what you're doing today?"

No, and there was a lot of 'em. You know, you look the country over, go down the Hardwick Road there. Just see how many little farms there is . . . well, it's more around through Woodbury there. We keep seein' 'em today. We'll say, "Well, there's a little farm could be made like ours." And . . . nobody wants to bother. What a sideline it would make—ya take anybody havin' a mail route or some work and still run a little farm like this, and he'd have two checks instead of the one, ya know. I don't know why nobody wants to bother. We do have quite a load. The little fella gets hurt a lot here, but we're still hangin' on. It don't seem they can drive us off here. The milk haulin' away's the worst. We have to give three dollars every other day, no matter how much milk we've got. Just to back and stop he asks three dollars where the other fella gets his for eighteen cents and that's our biggest thing. And of course we have to stay in under the milk inspection just the same, but we expect to do that. But this milk haulin', he gets eighteen cents and if he'd put that up to twenty cents for all of us, he'd get a lot more money than he does to get three dollars off us— that's the way I feel about it—and we'd feel much better, too.

"Was the quality of life when you were a young man any better than it is today? Do you feel that life is better or worse today than when you were a young man?"

Yes, I do. We've lost loyalty.

"Loyalty to what?"

Everything. We didn't use to have to have two or three witnesses on things. You and I could trade and it would be just

as bindin' as anything you could have. But we lost that. I don't know when it went nor how, but that's the part that I see has dropped the worst of anything. We have luxuries and a lot more than we did, but we ain't solid here anymore. You have to put everything down on paper and get it signed and then you ain't sure. But, that loyalty, I did hate to see it go here and it sure has. I don't know when it began, but that's the main thing I see different. We wouldn't want things to turn back here I guess, the roads especially.

"How do you feel about roads today and the maintenance of those roads as compared to what travel was like when you were a young man?"

Well, that's it. The cars have done it. That's the thing that's hurt us the most. Our little towns here are just wading in debt and what's done it is openin' these roads for winter travel with cars. We was getting on fine—town was outa debt and everything—until we had to open the roads. Sandin' and the next day they scrape it off and they put on more sand and another snowstorm will come and it's just beatin' 'em right out. We just can't keep up here. I don't know what's to happen, but all these little towns are in the same shape and it's gettin' quite terrible.

"What about transportation and the fact that now people are driving fast and moving from town to town, driving to Canada for the weekend? Compare this to what it was like when you were a young man."

I guess this is quite some different. If we got over to the first neighbor, we'd do well. We didn't go on long hikes, I can tell ya. No, especially in the winter.

"What did that mean then for you?"

Well, kept us quieted down now, in my mind. Sure, I think we was home and we was happy at the home; we weren't achin' to go anyplace. We was really happy right there. I don't like this wishin' you was in Connecticut when you're here and when you're down in Connecticut, wishin' you was in Vermont. You got an awful lot of people that's just like that. That's bad . . . that wanderlust gets on to you. We never had it. My brother and I run a farm for four years after we got sick of workin' out. We had a pretty good time and didn't make too much money. Then I went back to workin' out a little while and in 1918 I bought the place over here and then I was married in '21. We was there for forty-two years on that place, and we owned this one along with it for the last ten years or so, and we just retired from there out to here in 1961. This was just our size here— has been all along. We felt how lucky we were to have a little business just like this and be able to stay in or stay out. I smell out the door here and if the weather don't smell right, I come right back in and set down.

"How old are you now?"

Eighty-one. I'll be eighty-two come July. Eighty-one and a half—I don't see that one makes much difference; I don't pay much attention to that part of it. It's how I feel.

"Mrs. Urie, do you cook on the wood stove?"

I like to get my meals on a wood stove. We start it up every morning. I cook my meat and cook my vegetables on it, but I do my baking on the other one.

Mr. Urie: *That's two years younger'n I am. I used to say, "We'll see who lasts the longest," but I ain't said that in quite a little while—it's beating me.*

"What do you think is going to happen to Vermont?"

Mrs. Urie: *Well, I don't want too many outsiders to come up. I'd hate to see this little farm be sold and all the fields go for nothin'. I'd like to see the house kept up of course, but I'd like to see people farm the way we do.*

"What do you think will prohibit people from being able to farm?"

Mrs. Urie: *I don't think they want to work that hard. Well, it's the truth—they don't.*

Mr. Urie: *They say how hard we're workin'; now you see me choppin' wood up here. It's a pleasure. I'd rather go up there as to do anything else out. All by myself, I go up there and I have an awful good time till I get hungry. Then I come down. No! I enjoy my work—every bit of it.*

Mrs. Urie: *Why, I suppose people think it's awful hard. I'd help him hay—but it isn't to me.*

Mr. Urie: *She's always had to hay. At home she hayed.*

"You both really love life, don't you?"

Mr. Urie: *Well, why not?*

"I know. Why not? The Bible says why not, too."

Mr. Urie: *Lots of folk wouldn't think that's an easy job keepin' that driveway clean clear back to that car. Why, I can shovel more snow than any snowblow machine I've ever seen with that old red shovel over there. I went out there this morning—there's quite a little snow there. It was cold enough so's I had to work.*

Mrs. Urie: *Oh, the kids all get after us and they say, "Oh, why don't you get a snowblower?"*

Mr. Urie: *Yeah. Why don't you get a chain saw and why don't you get a this and that. And we'd be in worse shape than we was over on the other place there.*

Mrs. Urie: *So many people, they're perfectly able. Why, they won't even have a garden.*

Mr. Urie: *Won't raise a potato.*

Mrs. Urie: *And a garden—why it's the best therapy for any tension that there ever was.*

Mr. Urie: *We hay just as we did and we sugar just as we did. We got an outfit here that's workin'. They laugh at our size farm here, these fellas, but it's workin' and that's the main thing to my mind.*

"So many of the young people now in America are wanting to get back to exactly what you two are doing and have done. . . . I am here with a tape recorder because we respect what you two stand for . . ."

Mrs. Urie: *Have you read that book—the* Foxfire Book?

"That's what we're trying to do for Vermont! From all that you people are saying, we are trying to put together a book containing the best thoughts that people like you have to share. Are there many people like you left in the area?"

No, no. There's hardly any small farms. There was six in this milk route that had to pay the minimum instead of by the hundred pound. Now they're all doin' somethin' else, using it as a sideline. We don't have any sideline here. Yes, we do, too—all this poultry, the sugarin', and all that is a sideline, and then we sell Christmas trees and pulp and fireplace wood.

"Do you split the wood?"

Mr. Urie: *Oh, yeah. Sure.*

"And you cut the pulp?"

Yeah. I have to have six run of wood to keep this little stove goin'. And then there's six cords of three foot wood for the sugar house.

"Do you have a chain saw?"

Mr. Urie: *No.*

"How do you cut your wood?"

Mr. Urie: *With the old bow saw. Yeah, sure.*

"Really?"

Mr. Urie: *Sure.*

"Do you do it because you like it or because you can't afford a chain saw?"

Mr. Urie: *Because I like to.*

"Who helps you?"

Mr. Urie: *Nobody.*

"You cut six cords of wood . . . by yourself?"

Mr. Urie: *Sure. Sure. This year my son-in-law came over. He had a chain saw and his boy was home. They fell four trees for me and they cut it into four-foot blocks and then they went home and I split it. Then I put it up on my sawhorse and saw it twice in two. I can't stand machinery. That's why I got the old horse. I don't like machinery.*

"Why?"

Mr. Urie: *Don't start with me. A lawn mower—I can hardly coax it to go in the summertime. You take a chain saw in the winter. Why those fellas that mornin' they came over to cut my wood pulled on that old chain saw enough to cut a whole cord of wood there.*

"I spoke with a woman earlier today who said people didn't get as sick at the turn of the century as they do now. Did you find people got sick more in the early days, that there was more sickness when you were young?"

Mrs. Urie: *No, we hardly ever went to a doctor. People just weren't sick, that's all.*

Mr. Urie: *Simple livin', I think.*

Mrs. Urie: *I don't think they worried so much then. They didn't go at so fast a pace, you know.*

Mr. Urie: *Can't see where we're gittin'. We're always in a hurry, but we don't seem to be gettin' anyplace. I don't quite understand."*

New London, New Hampshire

Daisies

Blackwater River, New Hampshire

Mount Washington, New Hampshire

Acadia National Park, Maine

Land of the Pointed Firs

Maine's former Governor Percival Baxter tried unsuccessfully to con-
vince his legislature to create a state park around Mount Katahdin in
the Maine woods. After leaving office, he purchased the land himself
and gave what today is Baxter State Park to the people of Maine, under
the condition that the park would be forever wilderness. The park roads
are unpaved, the narrow "tote" road in places limited to 20 m.p.h., in
contrast to national park "speedways." Once logged for pulpwood, the
Baxter park forests have almost completely returned to the wilderness
envisioned by their donor—the wilderness experienced by Thoreau
and the early settlers who first saw the glow of the morning sun on the
summit of Mount Katahdin, highest point in Maine.

Mount Katahdin, Baxter State Park, Maine

Deer Isle, Maine

Bucksport, Maine

A Sampler of New England Life

TO GENERALIZE ABOUT New England life is a risky proposition. There is no common appellation for the various races, religions, and economic styles flourishing in this part of the world. "Proper Bostonians" may still head the Boston banks (because they still own them), but they are a small minority—even fewer in number than the flinty Vermont farmers whose accents are rapidly fading from the countryside. Few people have been here long enough to be considered "natives," and it would seem that for every impatient young person moving west for supposedly better economic opportunities, a replacement travels northeast from New York to escape the big-city competition.

New England is a kind of restless gathering place for a complex and diverse mixture of people who are loosely held together by strands of history, pride, and instinctive restraint and who advocate a better life. Despite a multitude of problems stirred up by their own competing desires, they are convinced that New England is a better place to live than anywhere else. It is not surprising that descendants of Pilgrims who arrived on the *Mayflower* are outnumbered by immigrants who came over in steerage and who later drove in from New York State.

Markers along the thin red-painted path of the Freedom Trail identify well-known revolutionary historical sites but strangely fail to point out that the Italian North End through which it twists and turns is itself a historical place over 300 years old. When the English founders of Boston who first settled the North End saw Irish move in, they must have felt it was the beginning of the end—the neighborhood was changing. Then Jews rented the small apartments wedged into narrow streets. The Italians followed. Each ethnic group in its own way created a true sense of community style not at all unlike the upper-class cohesiveness of either Beacon Hill or the old Back Bay. In some ways there is more integrity to the daily life of the North End because not only do the residents live there but they also work and play there. No public housing project or suburban development can boast of what the North End of Boston takes for granted.

New England's social diversity is a challenge to statisticians. This region has a relatively crime-free status, which is probably due to the fact that New England's environment is predominantly rural. Most of the population lives in homes scattered across the landscape or gathered in small factory towns and agricultural communities.

The rural environment does not seem to attract crime. Criminals apparently find that cities and wealthier areas like Cape Cod are more lucrative. Many Vermont towns have no police services at all, relying on the state police for emergencies.

The county of Fairfield in Connecticut is the wealthiest in New England—several of its towns are among the wealthiest in the United States. Almost all the homes in Greenwich, Connecticut, are worth more than $25,000—many of them on multiple-acre lots that exceed $250,000 in value. According to the Greenwich Chamber of Commerce: "The town stands alone, an emerald island of calm amidst a troubled sea of life's commoner annoyances." Greenwich has no industry to speak of and shares a scarcity of pollution and urban difficulties with other affluent commuter communities—Stamford, Norwalk, Darien, for example—that are linked with Manhattan by the asphalt and steel spine of Interstate 95 and the aging and money-losing Penn Central commuter railroad.

Executives in publishing, corporate business, banking, television, and advertising combine in a Fairfield County economic blockbuster which provides them with average incomes that far exceed the national average. Their buying power leads the state and the nation. In a state with the highest per capita annual income in the nation, a Fairfield County income of $50,000 is common. The median value of the homes is over $35,000, more than $10,000 greater than the value of homes in Hartford—the next richest Connecticut county—where firearms and insurance have created their own economic bonanza.

But there is a difference, and the economic gap between Fairfield and Hartford counties is illustrative of vast differences in the standard of living throughout New England. Where Fairfield has over 34,000 homes worth $50,000 or more, Hartford has less than 6,000. Where most Fairfield communities enjoy full employment and few social problems, Hartford communities have a minority population of twenty-two percent—largest in Connecticut—combined with one of the region's consistently highest unemployment rates because of the concentration of industry in government business. Many other New England single-industry towns poise on the brink of disaster brought on by an economic climate beyond their control.

The legislature of New Hampshire—officially the New Hampshire General Court—has 400 representatives and 24 senators, making it the third largest deliberative body in the western world, ranking after the British Parliament and the U.S. Congress.

New England has more representatives speaking for fewer people than any other region in the nation. Vermont is second to New Hampshire in representation. Maine is fourth, and tiny Rhode Island is sixth with 100 representatives for somewhat less than one-million people.

New Hampshire's legislators are among the lowest paid in the nation, receiving $100 a year plus a small graduated mileage allowance. They meet at Concord for only one regular session during their two-year term of office but often call special sessions for which they receive $3 a day expense money.

Meldrim Thomson, Jr., governor of New Hampshire, says his legislature is the "most democratic government in all fifty states." For all the governor's claims, however, most observers concede that the General Court is not as representative as it would appear since only the twenty-four senators pass on bills that come from the House. Many public hearings are held by only one senator. For years the average Granite State representative and senator have been in their mid-sixties and extremely conservative. Few of them face any real opposition in their "races" for election.

New Hampshire does not have a state income tax or a sales tax—the only state in the nation with neither. The little cash that New Hampshire does spend is raised by what local residents call "sin" taxes: revenue from state liquor stores, dog races, and horse races; cigarette taxes; and a state lottery.

But statistics do not tell the real story of New England. No "sampler of New England life" would be complete without an insight into the character of the people, because it is after all the people—as much as peculiar physical features—that make any region distinctive.

Gracious New England hospitality is openly extended to the visitor—but offered with restraint to those giving indications of staying. The casual visitor will not be aware of any reserve, but the visitor who decides to remain is never truly accepted even though he may be openly welcomed and find no doors closed to enjoyable social relationships.

In the Bennington, Vermont, *Banner* an obituary for a popular town selectman recounted in kindly detail the career of a man who had spent his entire life in a small neighboring town. A final sentence was revealing: "Although he was not a native of this town, we had begun to think of him as one of us." A search of village records uncovered the intriguing fact that he had arrived in town at the age of two weeks. In small New England communities it still takes a while to be accepted.

The *San Francisco Examiner* printed an article by New England native Dick Nolan, who went back for a visit in the summer of 1973 to try and recapture his past. "I went looking for roots, mine," he wrote. "Drunk with nostalgia (I am the last of the New England romantics) I wanted to see if the old road was still there . . . and perhaps some wisps and tatters of an awkward youth. . . .

"And there indeed it was, much as I had left it, except that the road had been paved, and on some of the meadowland rather elegant homes had been constructed, occupied by retired military men mostly, judged by parade ground neatness and the prevalent flagpoles."

In his wanderings Dick stopped in a small New Hampshire village and encountered again an attitude so familiar in rural New England—the forthright, honest nature of the rural New Englander.

"In a fever of remembering," he went on, "I wandered about the lanes and byways, and eventually came upon the apple place. There was a roadside sign that said, 'Apples.' Good New England economy with words. And off the road a large barn with another sign that said, 'Apples.'

"Inside the barn were the apples, as promised. Apples in boxes, apples in baskets, apples in brown paper bags of various dimensions. And in the middle of all this sweet-smelling opulence a table with a large glass jar on it half filled with currency and coins.

"The sign on the table said, 'Help Yourself. Leave Money in Jar.'

"Fresh from California, where wary shopkeepers require a complete dossier plus fingerprints before they'll accept a $5 check, I found myself immeasurably warmed by the lonely table, the treasure jar, and the sign that proclaimed the old virtues as I remembered them. The apple man, whoever he was and wherever he was, made my day. He was operating on the assumption that I, and all like me that passed that way, were honest!"

But New Englanders can also be stubborn, obstinate, and contentious. Maine and New Hampshire have been arguing over the boundaries of the territorial waters of New Hampshire for years. New Hampshire may be a bit sensitive about the problem, however, since of all the coastal New England states, it has the smallest access to the ocean.

And so in January 1973 the controversy flared again when Maine resource enforcement officers hauled a New Hampshire lobsterman into district court at Kittery, Maine, and charged him with trapping in Maine waters without a license. The lobsterman's plea that he was fishing in New Hampshire's waters fell on deaf ears. He was fined $50.

Hearing of the case, Governor Thomson of New Hampshire promptly requested his legislature to pass a bill extending the state's boundaries to a line 200 miles east of the New Hampshire shoreline. This new boundary would put several offshore islands and a good chunk of ocean within New Hamp-

shire's jurisdiction and out of reach of Maine's authority. At the same time, according to Governor Thomson, the move would keep Russian fishermen away from American lobsters.

The islands under contention have been considered part of Maine ever since 1635. The difference of opinion lies in whether the line connecting harbor midpoints mentioned in the English king's order of 1740 is straight or curved. New Hampshire insists that simple logic dictates a straight line. Maine asserts that if the king had meant straight, he would have said straight and relies on the curved line shown on U.S. charts of 1920. Maine calls New Hampshire's interpretation of the old mapped line "nothing more than bald assertions based solely on fanciful wish" and gleefully offers in evidence a distinctly curved line shown on the 1973 New Hampshire official state highway map. The U.S. Geological Survey spokesman says it can find no documentary evidence for either a straight or a curved line.

The controversy intensified in June 1973 when New Hampshire's errant—but persistent—lobsterman was arrested again. This time angry Maine wardens tried to confiscate his boat and traps. Governor Thomson considered calling out the National Guard and cried that "Maine has apparently declared war on us!" He sent state wardens out in retaliation, and at night they cut the buoys of more than 200 Maine lobster traps in the disputed seas. They were valued at $3,000.

Kenneth M. Curtis, governor of Maine, immediately telegraphed Governor Thomson: "This is to notify you that until such time as this matter is finally resolved . . . Maine will begin immediately to enforce Maine law in all areas on the Maine side of the seaward boundary."

Maine's commissioner of sea and shore announced, "We are urging our fishermen to restrain themselves." He further said he did not anticipate any violent reactions. In one amusing incident, however, the New Hampshire state flag that had flown for many years over a small unoccupied island in the no-man's sea mysteriously disappeared.

The lobsterman filed suit against Maine, claiming piracy on the high seas. New Hampshire went to the U.S. Supreme Court for a ruling to open up the small triangular offshore area that, because of the projected boundaries of Maine and Massachusetts, is New Hampshire's sole access to the sea. Governor Thomson said, "Our contention is that what we start with we want to end up with seaward. We have 17.3 miles of shoreline and what we want to end up with, 200 miles out, is 17.3 miles."

So the arguments are flung back and forth as each side proclaims the rightness of its case, creating a situation that will probably continue indefinitely until either Maine or New Hampshire gives in or the Supreme Court decides the issue.

Perhaps most characteristic of New England is the fierce independence of a people who by their own will and strength, their persistence and their pride in themselves, have created a spirit found nowhere else in this nation. This is perhaps illustrated by the Vermonter who had bought an old, run-down farm and worked hard getting it back in operating condition.

When it was in pretty good working shape, the local minister happened to stop by for a call. He congratulated the farmer on the results of his labors, remarking that it was wonderful what God and man could do together.

"Ayeh, p'raps it is," the farmer said. "But you should have seen this place when God was running it alone."

Maybe the essence of New England is, as Vermont legislator and humorist Allen Foley would say, all part of New England wit and wisdom, developed by attempting to tame a stubborn, unpredictable, but astonishingly beautiful land.

Farmhouse near Rumford, Maine

Pemaquid Light, Pemaquid Point, Maine

Wiscasset, Maine

Bar Harbor, Maine

Lumbering, Maine woods

Shadblow

Frenchman Bay and Cadillac Mountain, Maine

The Atlantic Shore

Nantucket Island, Massachusetts

Paving stones, Nantucket Island, Massachusetts

Land of Two Worlds

ALLEN FOLEY, Vermont legislator and humorist, told this story at a Chamber of Commerce annual dinner in Bennington, Vermont. An out-of-state visitor from the big city, stopping at a remote dairy farm, inquired of the farmer if he wasn't sometimes lonesome out here? The Vermonter replied quite honestly, "I don't know what you're talking about."

"Well," the visitor continued, "I was just wondering if sometimes you didn't wish you were nearer the center of things."

The Vermont farmer, obviously unaware he was too far away from anyplace important, replied, "Mister, I'm exactly five miles from Norwich. And exactly five miles from Strafford. I'm exactly one-hundred-and-sixty miles from Boston and one-hundred-and-sixty miles from Montreal. I don't see how a feller could be much nearer the center of things."

The Vermonter could have been speaking for all New Englanders, those residents of the six northeastern states whose provincialism is the one common trait bridging widespread economic and political differences between lobstermen and bank presidents. If they agree on anything, it is that New England is at the center of everything worth mentioning. If they had to choose the only place in the world they preferred to live, their common choice would be New England.

Radio may have blended such things as the distinctive speech patterns of the Connecticut Nutmeggers and the Vermont Green Mountain boys (and television has most everyone talking like midwestern TV news commentators), but it has affected little else. Traditional homespun philosophies are still expressed on the village commons. Regionalism is as much the life-style of New England as it was when Calvin Coolidge took the presidential oath of office by kerosene lantern in the small Vermont cottage of his father.

New England is to a considerable extent still a small town, albeit spread over six states. Perhaps the key to understanding these six states is the realization that this landscape, formed during the glacial age, has changed little since the ice melted —and a few old-timers have changed even less. They have done little more to the land than erect villages at appropriate sites, although things did get out of hand in Boston.

New England is handicapped by a harsh climate featuring weeks of overcast skies; hot, humid summers; and long cold winters broken by frequent storms often covering the entire region with a deep mantle of snow. Vermont and New Hampshire may be buried in snow for three, four, or even five months of the year, and Connecticut may be paralyzed by destructive ice storms. Maine, with the most rugged shoreline of any maritime state, never seems free of chill ocean winds. One geographer has noted that if America had been settled first on the Pacific Coast, in all probability, New England might not have been discovered yet. Along the Connecticut River valley in southern Vermont, a village sign attests to the climate of New England: "Nine months of hard winter. Three months of poor skiing." A disappointed visitor who asked about spring was told it occurred Tuesday.

Yet, few residents move away, even when improved wages and job opportunities beckon. To a considerable extent, the shift of young people from rural hometowns to big-city jobs does not occur because small manufacturing is still an important economic fact of life in hundreds of tiny villages tucked into narrow valleys carved out of glacial moraines. The boy who leaves the farm in all probability only moves as far as the nearest town for steady work. The pattern of small industries, which remain from the days when waterwheel power determined the factory site, today still governs the growth or death of many small communities now utilizing power generated by nuclear reactors. In many ways it is this unique mix of very old and very new that characterizes New England and makes generalized observations difficult.

All over the countryside are the remnants of the past—the sights that make New England so unique—the covered bridges and slender white church spires, the stone walls surrounding ghost farms abandoned 100 years ago, and the early colonial residential architecture still dominating many communities, particularly along the southeast coast where Cape Cod saltbox houses perch jauntily atop grassy sand dunes like a row of houses in a Monopoly game. Forests of rotting stubs in tidal mud identify long-abandoned shipyards where Yankee Clippers were launched to carry the varied products of New England to the Old World and beyond.

And, as they have always done, lobster pots clutter every pier, and bobbing bright-colored buoys are sprinkled over lobster beds beneath the sea. Sleepy, quiet coves shelter fragile boats of hardy fishermen who harvest the rich fishing grounds of shallow ocean shoals a day's trip offshore.

The old towns still remain, but their quaint charm is slowly but inexorably dying. The ancient cannon and stiff statues commemorating almost-forgotten wars are removed from the town Green, which is then paved over for parking. The winding road into town is straightened and widened into a highway. The old merchants retire, and new stores join others in the slick shopping mall constructed on the edge of town. The town center slowly dies as terminal cancer of the heart spreads outward until the city core is dead. Were it not for the actions of alert historical societies, few physical symbols of historical traditions would have been saved to remind visitors that New England is where American independence was born.

But much that has made the character of New England so distinctive is disappearing. The rugged, individualistic New Englander, still found in a few remote villages, is a dying breed, so rapidly diluted by New Yorkers and Bostonians moving upcountry for the summer that distinguishing characteristics are melting into qualities common to any small town in the West.

Cultural isolation once guaranteed by narrow mountain roads has been shattered by interstate freeways bringing the problems of downtown Boston within two hours of farms in the White Mountains of New Hampshire.

The characteristic humor of rural Vermont, New Hampshire, and Maine is difficult to find today. The same old stories are told again and again by residents who see their world fading all too rapidly.

And there is the fast-disappearing stereotyped New Englander, flinty and silent, prone to quick and allegedly unpremeditated comebacks to innocent queries. Allen Foley tells this story: a car approaches a fork in the road where two signs both point to White River Junction. The driver asks the old Vermonter standing nearby, "Does it make any difference which road I take to White River Junction?"

With all the traditional independence and taciturnity he can muster, the old-timer replies, "Not to me, it don't."

111

But today the Vermonter with country traits of thrift and independence is virtually a stranger in a state buying railroads and initiating statewide zoning laws to cope with a dying dairy industry, unsightly tourist developments, and "second home" buyers who purchase the farmland almost before the cows are milked. Emotional restraint is no longer a regional characteristic. The struggle among citizen conservation groups, farmer lobbies, land developers, industry, opportunistic politicians, and oil-well drillers is changing not only the landscape but the people as well.

New England is a land of two worlds. One world is the aristocracy born of history and revolution, rich from industry and inheritance, loyal to traditions and ancestors. They may not have arrived on the *Mayflower,* but at the very least they are the children of those who arrived shortly after.

Another world is perhaps ninety percent of the population —the French Canadians, Irish Catholics, Italians, Blacks, and Latin Americans among others. This is the world of the working class—blue and white collar—and the intelligentsia who make Cambridge and Boston the greatest brain repositories in the United States.

Sarah Orne Jewett, Maine's foremost author at the turn of the century, reflected this contradiction between two worlds in her first book, *Deephaven,* written in 1877, where she sentimentalizes the summer experiences of two proper, young Bostonians on a quaint summer retreat to an imaginary New England seaport village. It is synonymous with many towns in New England today.

In the preface to the 1893 edition she reflects on the revolution in rural New England that had occurred in the short years since the first publication of *Deephaven:*

"The short lifetime of this little book has seen great changes in the conditions of provincial life in New England. Twenty years ago, or a little more, the two heroines whose simple adventures are here described might well have served as types of those pioneers who were already on the eager quest for rural pleasures. Twenty years ago, our fast-growing New England cities, which had so lately been but large towns, full of green gardens and quiet neighborhoods, were just beginning to be overcrowded and uncomfortable in summer. . . . This presently showed itself to be of unsuspected force and significance: it meant something more than the instinct for green fields and hills and the seashore; crowded towns and the open country were to be brought together in new association and dependence upon each other. . . . Old farmhouses opened their doors to the cheerful gayety of summer; the old jokes about the respective aggressions and ignorances of city and country cousins gave place to new compliments between the summer boarder and his rustic host. . . .

"In those days, if one had just passed her twentieth year, it was easy to be much disturbed by the sad discovery that certain phases of provincial life were fast waning in New England. . . . Tradition and time-honored custom were to be swept away together by the irresistible current. Character and architecture seemed to lose individuality and distinction. The new riches of the country were seldom very well spent in those days; the money that the tourist or summer citizen left behind him was apt to be used to sweep away the quaint houses, the roadside thicket, the shady woodland, that had lured him first; and the well-filled purses that were scattered in our country's first great triumphal impulse of prosperity often came into the hands of people who hastened to spoil instead of to mend the best things that their village held. It will remain for later generations to make amends for the sad use of riches after the war, for our injury of what we inherited, for the irreparable loss of certain ancient buildings which would have been twice as interesting in the next century as we are just beginning to be wise enough to think them in this."

Robert Horn, the president of St. Francis College in Biddeford, Maine, commented on the social power of Jewett prose: "Deephaven society may venerate and imitate the past, but it never quite measures up; it is dry-rotting as surely as the wharves that once symbolized its involvement in the wider world, and is about as aware of it." The New England of Sarah Jewett's novel could be the New England of today.

Two of the best things money can buy are space and solitude—and they are expensive. Most of the space and solitude in New England have already been purchased, and little remains for the average worker or vacationer. Selfish exploitation of the natural beauty around New England lakes and along the Atlantic shore for the benefit of the private landowner and the tourist is a harsh commentary on a region that rushes to preserve history.

While in theory the seashore belongs to everyone, access to the water—or even the sight of it—is impossible along hundreds of miles of ocean shore and beach in Connecticut, Massachusetts, and Maine and inland on the lakes of Vermont and New Hampshire. No one can really be kept out of the water, but private property owners can—and do—make it impossible to get there. Even parking cars nearby is prohibited in many areas under threat of stiff fines or being towed away. The visitor is not wanted. Keep out! Or as one Connecticut sign warns: "Tresspassers will be eaten!"

Public ownership of still-open land would appear to be the only alternative. An extension of Cape Cod National Seashore northward to include all the Maine coast without the gerrymandering that makes Maine's Acadia National Park such a shameful compromise is imperative. There has long been a proposal to establish a Connecticut River Valley National Recreation Area to include all the river valley from its source to Long Island Sound. Considerable political vision and geographical pride will be necessary to protect these national treasures in the years to come.

Roses, Wenham, Massachusetts

Anne W. Simon has published her lone plea to save Martha's Vineyard, in Massachusetts, from the ravages of tourists and rapacious landowners. Elizabeth Yates has written her eloquent call to save New Hampshire's Sandwich Notch from the bulldozers of unresponsive speculative land developers. Where is the book to save the rest of New England?

It is clear this has been an on-going process. Ralph Waldo Emerson commented in 1842 on the coming of the railroad to New England, and with it the despoiling of the land.

"I hear the whistle of the locomotive in the woods. Wherever that music comes it has its sequel. It is the voice of the civility of the nineteenth century saying, 'Here I am.' It is interrogative; it is prophetic; and this Cassandra is believed: 'Whew! Whew! Whew! How is real estate here in the swamp and wilderness? Ho for Boston! Whew! Whew! Down with that forest on the side of the hill. I want ten thousand chestnut sleepers. I want cedar posts, and hundreds of thousands of feet of boards. Up! My master of oak and pine! You have waited long enough —a good part of a century in the wind and stupid sky. Ho for axes and saws, and away with me to Boston! Whew! Whew! I will plant a dozen houses on this pasture next moon, and a village anon; and I will sprinkle yonder square mile with white houses like the broken snowbanks that strow it in March.' "

Control of state lands and ownership of private property does not carry with it the right to allow destruction of scenic or recreational areas contrary to the long-term best interests of the public. The natural beauty, open space, and historical sites of New England are irreplaceable and belong to all the people of the United States. Yet in the case of proposals for Connecticut River valley parks, for legislative restrictions of land development on the Massachusetts islands of Martha's Vineyard and Nantucket, and for national park and wilderness tracts throughout the region, intense opposition is heard from affected private property owners who have effectively quashed important long-range land-preservation proposals that were designed to permanently protect the scenic values and natural beauty of New England.

Local communities along the Connecticut River between the Connecticut towns of Old Saybrook and East Haddam where national recreation areas are proposed reject any form of federal ownership or regulation of open space. Their spokesmen are quoted as "dreading the spectre of hordes of tourists clogging access roads, overrunning parking areas and campsites, and leaving behind piles of litter."

Ellsworth Grant, mayor of West Hartford, Connecticut, says, "Instead of federal controls, they favor a state-local conservation compact, with powers to freeze present zoning along the river as far back as the visible ridgelines of the surrounding hills, in order to preserve forever the ecology, scenic, and historic values."

Even the mayor knows zoning of any kind is very temporary. Zoning protects nothing "forever." Since zoning, subject to change at the whim of opportunistic politicians, protects only the speculative property owner, it would appear that local residents are usually more interested in preserving future rights for resale of their property than they are in preserving the scenic heritage of the area.

Public acquisition of the land by purchase or gift can provide permanent protection. Competent management of publicly owned land will effectively prevent overuse by outdoor enthusiasts. It would not be an exaggeration to envision all of New England as a great "parkland" with future community development subservient to natural beauty and open space amenities. Surely the magnificent natural attributes and revo-

lutionary events that have occurred on this land offer sufficient rationale for a special kind of protection.

The popular actor William Gillette, who immortalized Sherlock Holmes on the stage, was so disturbed over the misuse of the Connecticut River valley and the future status of his palatial home overlooking the river at Hadlyme, Connecticut, that in his will he specifically instructed the executors of his estate to see to it that the property did not fall into the "possession of some blithering saphead who has no conception of where he is or with what surrounded." Today Gillette's "castle" is a Connecticut state park.

The unfinished Interstate 93 will be an unsheathed knife twisted into New Hampshire's famed Franconia Notch. Tourist litter scattered along the wound already opened into the fragile White Mountains north of Woodstock is testimony to the criminal acts of desecration perpetuated by a recreation industry recklessly chain-sawing "yo-yo" ski runs out of upland forests and strip-mining irreplaceable natural beauty along the valley floor to accommodate tourist ghettos and ill-conceived exhibition cages for trained bears. In the name of "jobs and economic development," the shortsighted New Hampshire highway department is willing to sacrifice even the Old Man of the Mountains, surely the most famous landmark in New England, if they can thereby squeeze a few more cars and dollars into the area. When the Old Man collapses, shaken down by road-builders' dynamite, a responsible land ethic might emerge, but it will be too late.

The Green Mountain men of Vermont were the first to see the danger and demand strong state land-zoning laws to preserve the beauty of their countryside against second-home sprawl and irresponsible progress.

Aggressive members of the Sierra Club and the National Audubon Society, joined by a hundred local citizen environmental groups, have opposed those who would violate the land. They stand together in total opposition to further economic and cultural rape of New England.

As increasing swarms of visitors engulf New England in every season of the year, it becomes increasingly prudent to ask "How many is too many?" A slowdown in the rate of tourist growth and establishment of optimum levels of visitor population to maintain the unique quality of life that is still a part of New England must become tomorrow's political platform. Continued expansion of tourist facilities will eventually destroy the desirable attributes of New England that have attracted visitors to these shores since the Pilgrims first landed by accident. Time is running out. Lake Mascoma in western New Hampshire is already polluted, possibly beyond saving. Millions of visitors have trampled Henry Thoreau's Walden Pond into a dreary desert of raw earth only barely disguised by winter snows. On Cape Cod the deep wells that are the traditional sources of fresh water have become saline because heavy tourist demands in summer months lower the water table, which allows ocean water to seep in. The wells will soon run dry—or become too salty to drink from.

Even the birthplace of the American hamburger, Louis' Lunch in New Haven, Connecticut, may be swallowed up by a twelve-story medical complex the city says it needs more urgently. Hamburgers are still sold at Louis' the same way they were first served in 1900—stashed between two pieces of toast without any modern embellishments. As a significant historical site, Louis' place may be almost as important to some people as Concord Bridge.

With the loss of historical sites, traditions, unique institutions, pastoral scenery, wild mountains, and narrow gulfs, the uniqueness of New England will become the province of novels and history books. The distinctive life-style described by hundreds of inspired residents in every possible medium has already—sadly—become only a memory in much of New England. Without the white church steeples, still a reassuring sight above the elm- and maple-shaded streets, many communities might have been transplanted from Iowa or Oregon with little change.

Alistair Cooke might have been thinking of New England when he spoke about his impressions of the United States to Associated Press columnist Jay Sharbutt. "And now this country is disturbing," he said. "It's upsetting to me."

"How has it changed?" asked Sharbutt.

"The thing I've noticed is that it's almost impossible to identify a place the moment you get out of a plane. It's just miles of motelsville, secondhand car lots, hamburger stands, the refuse and litter. It's not a question of saving what's left; it's more of recovering what's lost. It's gone at such a speed."

To suggest that New England should remain the same—totally unchanged by yearly waves of summer visitors, idealistic college youths, and escapees from the urban congestion of New York and Boston—may be asking for cultural stagnation in place of a vibrant, exciting community. But growth without wise consideration of the limits, progress without careful understanding of the consequences, and profits without long-range appreciation of the costs will destroy a way of life most of us desire—a life-style that is still New England's to cherish.

Perhaps half the residents of New England are originally from somewhere else. Many live in the country or in small rural towns still boasting a town Green and the town meeting. They share a common life-style, even if it is somewhat disguised by wide differences in income and various degrees of religious and ethnic intolerance. In this regard New England is little different from any other section of the country.

But common traits confirm tradition and define a people.

The soul common to all the six states of New England and unique in the nation is the past—the historic link with our pioneering ancestors and the nation they began. It is the land—the scenic stage—upon which the revolutionary history of the United States was enacted.

Almost from the moment visitors driving east on Interstate 90 cross the boundary of Massachusetts, they are surrounded by beauty and history, by an environment seriously damaged only in parts but still grand enough to excite the most jaded and steeped in tradition, sufficient to sway the most hostile of critics. It is a land to love.

The first New England whaling ship crossed the equator on the same day anxious Minutemen took their bold stand on the Lexington Green. New Englanders have always been a mixture of the adventurous and the brave. Now they face another adventure—the challenge of responsibly controlling their environment to preserve its natural beauty and its historical heritage. This is what life in New England today is all about.

New England is not New Hampshire, Maine, Boston, or Greenwich. Neither is it autumn foliage bus tours, chef's special seafood plates, county fairs, and flea markets. It is not the Maine wilderness around Moosehead Lake or the Hartford slums that still remain even after attempts at urban renewal. It is not the serene quiet of a Maine lobster cove or the typically urban welter of Boston streets. It is not the Boston Pops, Harvard Square, or McDonald's lighted flagpole. It is not even the swan boats floating in Boston Common Garden, the first dawn light shining on the summit of Maine's Mount Katahdin, a Rhode Island clambake, art on the village green, or a lighthouse in the night.

New England is the wonderful dream of men and women who landed on these shores and built it, who died in defense of it, who exploit it with skill, and live here simply because they love it.

Heritage Plantation, Sandwich, Cape Cod, Massachusetts

Provincetown, Cape Cod, Massachusetts

Gloucester, Massachusetts

Gloucester, Massachusetts

Gloucester, Massachusetts

Nauset Beach, Cape Cod, Massachusetts

Cape Cod Light